Th

Cookbook

Introduction

Are you looking for a much healthier alternative to deep-frying your favorite foods in unhealthy oils?

There are many reasons as to why someone might look for a way to turn their favorite, unhealthy foods into something that's not only delicious but something that's not going to clog their arteries and cause more health concerns than they already have. Many turn to baking in the oven. But did you know there's a much better, time-saving way to get those crunchy fries, fried chicken pieces, and even homemade potato chips that will use even less oil?

It's one of the latest kitchen inventions that allow you to cook without having to use the stove or oven. The air fryer imitates the motions found in a traditional fryer packed with oil, but it uses air instead of harmful oils to cook your food to perfection. In this book, I'm going to teach you all about air fryers, why you should be using one, and then provide you with recipes for breakfast, lunch, dinner, and even snacks that are all cooked without using tons of oil!

And just in case you're having trouble with your air fryer, there's a chapter about that, too.

So let's get started with how you can start using your air fryer today to make your life so much easier!

Chapter One - What Is An Air Fryer?

Hot air fryers are the newest invention for the kitchen since the 1970's creation of the slow cooker and the microwave. They're ingenious machines that allow you to fry, roast, and grill without needing to use excessive amounts of fat or oil, yet you still get the same deep-fried taste and texture without all that grease!

The secret to hot air fryers is their design. They're made to circulate very hot air in a fashion that mimics the actual motion and flow of heat currents in a boiling pot in order to crisp the outside of the food while it cooks the inside. There are some air fryers that also come with a grilling element in order to add crispiness and browning to the outside of your food.

So how does it compare to deep-fat frying?

The air-fried food is going to taste a little bit different from the deep-fried food, but most who rave about these kitchen appliances state the air-fried food tastes *better* than the fried foods they normally eat. No longer do you have to taste sodden-grease food that will sink to the pit of your stomach like a brick. Still, the taste is similar enough to fried foods without the awful cleanup and the heavy oil smell throughout your home. It's a lot less work, which means you get to enjoy fried foods more often! Not to mention the health benefits, too.

On the surface, it might look like hot air frying machines take a lot longer to make a batch of your favorite homemade foods, like twenty-five minutes to air fry fries rather than eight minutes of deep frying, but remember you don't have to wait for the air fryer to warm up as much or cool down before you are able to clean it up. Not to mention the outright hassle of having to clean up all that oil afterward. As much as people love deep-fried foods in oil, most of them don't cook it at home simply due to the hassle of it.

Hot air frying actually eliminates all of those hassles.

In addition to eliminating the hassle, hot air fryers allow you to consume your favorite fried foods, even if you have a health condition that prohibits you from doing so! In fact, hot air frying is actually a *healthy* way of eating. You use a lot less oil with hot air frying, which leads to a much healthier diet. In addition, you get to experiment with many different types of oils, such as walnut or avocado oil, which are healthier for you than other vegetable oils.

One of the other benefits of using a hot air fryer is that it's a lot safer than deep-fat frying on your stovetop. Hot oil burns from frying on the stovetop are actually a common cause of hospital admissions. There are over 2,600 fires a year attributed to deep fat frying in the home. Frying that way causes over a thousand casualties and twelve fatalities ever year.

Hot air frying reduces the risk of fried food cooking by a significant amount. It's so easy even a young teenager can do it! It's just as easy as using a toaster oven or a microwave, and it makes a fireman's life a lot easier.

If you're convinced that hot air frying is for you, keep reading to figure out what you should look for when it comes to purchasing one.

What Do I Look For?

Just as any other purchase, knowing the options that are available to you when it comes to a hot air fryer is the better way to making a good purchasing decision. Most hot air fryers will use the same technology and have similar features. All of them use hot air circulation in order to cook the food, so there isn't any difference in air fryers when it comes to design.

However, there are some different options out there when it comes to hot air fryers. Some features you may want to consider before you purchase one are as follows:

1. **Size:** It's imperative you make sure your countertop has the right amount of space to store your air fryer while you're using it.

2. **Wattage:** It's also important to make sure your kitchen outlet will support an 800-1400 watt appliance to avoid the risk of an electrical fire.

3. **Capacity:** Understanding the amount of food and the types of food you're going to be cooking is important when you go to purchase your air fryer. Typically, an air fryer will have the capacity to cook anywhere from 1.8 to 2.5 pounds of food, which is good for cooking fries and chicken drumsticks. However, if you believe you're going to be cooking an entire turkey, chicken or a larger meal, then you'll need a larger air fryer.

4. **Settings:** Figuring out the different settings that are available to you on your air fryer is going to help you make the proper decision. Most of the air fryers on the market will reach 360 degrees and come with a timer to make cooking easy. However, depending on the model and brand, the air fryer may not become as hot as you need to cook the types of foods you'd like to prepare. Be sure to

read reviews and the instructions before you purchase the air fryer.

5. **Other Features:** Some air fryers will come with the ability to cook two different food items at a time by having levels or baskets. This makes cooking things like fish and chips a lot easier, but it might not be necessary for those who want to use their air fryer for the occasional batch of fries or fried wings.

If you're someone who greatly enjoys fried foods, then a hot air fryer appliance might be your best kitchen appliance purchase yet! In the following chapter, we're going to explore the different benefits of owning an air fryer in more detail.

Chapter Two - Why Use One?

It's no secret that air fryers make your life easier and your food healthier, but how? Well, they can do just about anything. They can fry your favorite batch of fries or wings, grill a salmon filet to perfection, bake just about anything, and roast your favorite dish in less time than it would take in the oven. They're equipped with plastic and metal materials that will last you quite some time, too.

If you're worried about how heavy the air fryer will be, avoid hazards by using cooking gloves or pot holders while you move the air fryer. If you're worried about children, always make sure the air fryer is out of reach and in a safe area to cook, just like any other kitchen countertop appliance.

So why use one in the first place?

No Mess

With air fryers, you won't have to add extra oil to the food, which means less oil to clean up. All the ingredients are cooked with hot air and offer you the same or similar taste to oily fried foods. The best part about not having to use the oil is never having to clean all of it up afterward, and you won't have greasy stains on your fingers or your napkins. In fact, most air fryers call for using no oil, but when it does call for a little oil, you add it to the food rather than the air fryer.

Many people love the idea of eating a healthier version of the fried foods they once loved. The best part about the air fryer is the fact that it doesn't use oil, which means less of a mess and healthier foods. If you decide to prepare a dish with oil, be sure you use homemade foods rather than pre-heated foods. The appliance's manual will tell you which oils are appropriate for your air fryer.

Healthier

One of the biggest qualities your air fryer will offer is the healthier options for dishes. In comparison to other types of fryers on the market, air fryers are designed specifically to operate without fattening oils and to make food that has up to eighty percent less fat than food cooked with a conventional fryer.

Air fryers are able to help you lose the weight you've been struggling to toss. They will allow you to eat foods you once found were off the menu with your diet, allowing you to proverbially have your cake and eat it, too. You can still have fried dishes, but at the same time, you'll be conserving on calories and saturated fat.

Time-Saver

If you're someone who's on a tight schedule, like most, then you might want to consider using an air fryer. Within a few minutes, you'll have a crunchy batch of fries for lunch or some crispy chicken tenders for dinner. The air fryer is great for those who are constantly on the go and don't have a lot of time to prepare meals. With most air fryers, fries can be made in twelve minutes. Don't forget that they require less cleanup time, too!

Many Features

Air fryers come with different features, but the main ones are temperature and a timer. The temperature in an air fryer is almost instantaneous, but if you're starting the air fryer when it's been sitting for quite some time, just add three minutes to your cooking time. Air fryers are equipped with adjustable temperature controls that let you set the temperature for different meals. Most of them will go up to two hundred to three hundred degrees. And because they can cook foods at record times, they come with a timer that is able to be preset up to thirty minutes.

You can also check the progress of your meal without messing up the set time. Just pull out the pan and the fryer pauses heating! Once you put the pan back in, the fryer will start heating again. Once the meal is done and the timer has run out, the fryer alerts you with a sound. But just in case you miss that, the fryer automatically shuts off to prevent foods from burning and overcooking.

In addition to time and temperature, there's also the food separator option. Some air fryers will come with baskets that allow you to prepare frozen chicken nuggets and French fries at the same time or any other type of meal with two components. You don't have to worry about the flavors of the foods mixing, either!

One option that's beneficial and you might want to make sure your air fryer has is a built-in air filter that eliminates unwanted vapors and food odors from permeating your household. You don't have to smell like your favorite fried foods any longer. The air filter diffuses the hot oil steam and allows you to enjoy a fresh smelling kitchen with delicious foods.

Cleaning Is a Breeze

No longer do you need to fret after you've made lunch or dinner. Air fryers were specifically designed for hassle-free cleaning. The parts of your air fryer are made of non-stick materials, preventing foods from sticking to surfaces that make it harder to clean. It's recommended that you soak certain components before you clean them. All parts, like the grill and basket, are removable and dishwasher safe. After the ingredients are cooked, you can just put the parts in the dishwasher for easy cleanup!

Just remember you should always use detergents specialized in dissolving oil. In addition, leave the pan to soak in water for a few minutes before you put it in the dishwasher, and avoid using any metal utensils while you're cleaning to prevent scratches and scuffs on the material. Always allow your air fryer to cool half an hour before you clean it, too.

Cost-Effective

Air fryers seem like they cost more than most kitchen appliances, but the truth is that they use a lot less electricity than your stovetop and they will save you a ton in medical costs when you're eating a healthier diet. They save you time and money.

There are numerous benefits to using an air fryer and they far outweigh any negative aspects.

In the next chapter, we're going to explore breakfast recipes to get you started with your new air fryer.

Chapter Three – Breakfast Recipes

If you're trying to change your breakfast routine to something healthier, such as some grilled tomatoes or maybe a frittata, your air fryer can help you with that. You can even make healthier French fries to enjoy in the morning if you want to break completely out of the box! This chapter has ten recipes that will surely make your morning a little brighter and healthier at the same time.

Morning French Fries

Serves: 1

Ingredients

- 9 oz. Potatoes
- 1 tsp. Duck Fat

Directions

1. Wash and peel the potatoes and cut them into slices.

2. Put the fries into the fry pan with a teaspoon of duck fat, according to the manufacturer's instructions on how to use oil or fat in the air fryer. Cook for half an hour.

3. If you're using a basket-type air fryer, put the duck fat into a microwave safe bowl and heat it for ten to fifteen seconds in the microwave. Toss the potatoes in the fat and cook for twenty to twenty-five minutes. Begin at 320 degrees Fahrenheit, and then halfway

through, raise the temperature to 350 degrees Fahrenheit.

4. Serve them hot.

Air Grilled Tomatoes

Serves: 2

Ingredients

- 2 Tomatoes
- Herbs of Your Choice
- Cooking Spray
- Pepper

Directions

1. Wash your tomatoes and cut them in half. Turn them over and spray the bottoms very lightly with the cooking spray.

2. Turn the halves with the cut side up and spray the tops with a spritz of cooking spray. Sprinkle with the pepper and herbs.

3. Put the tomatoes in the top tray of your air fryer and turn it on for twenty minutes. If you're using a basket-type

fryer, stick them in at 320 degrees Fahrenheit for twenty minutes without a preheat time.

4. After twenty minutes have passed, check for doneness. This is going to vary depending on the size of your tomatoes and how many you're cooking at once. If they need a few more minutes, go ahead and give them ten more minutes.

Air Fried Potato Hash

Serves: 4

Ingredients

- 1 ½ lbs. Potatoes
- 2 tsp. Duck Fat
- 1 Onion
- ½ Green Bell Pepper
- ½ tsp. Savory Seasoning
- ½ Thyme
- ½ tsp. Black Pepper
- 1 tsp. Salt Substitute
- 1 C. Egg Substitute

Directions

1. Melt the duck fat your air fryer for two minutes.

2. Peel and dice the onion. Wash and seed the green pepper and then dice

it. Add the pepper to the onion in the air fryer and cook for five minutes.

3. Wash the potatoes, peel them, and dice them into small cubes. Add them to the air fryer along with the seasonings. Set the timer for half an hour and cook.

4. Meanwhile, spray a nonstick cooking pan with some cooking spray and grind a little pepper on it. Allow the pepper to heat for a minute to incorporate the flavor and pour the egg into the pan. Take it out of the pan and chop it up. Set it aside.

5. Once the timer beeps, add the egg to the potatoes and cook another five minutes.

6. Serve hot with sliced fresh tomatoes or mushrooms.

French Toast Sticks

Serves: 2

Ingredients

- 4 Slices of Bread
- 2 Tbsp. Butter
- 2 Eggs, Beaten
- Salt
- Nutmeg
- Cinnamon
- Ground Cloves
- Icing Sugar

Directions

1. Preheat your air fryer to 320 degrees Fahrenheit.

2. Beat the eggs in a bowl and sprinkle them with salt, a little cinnamon, and a pinch of nutmeg and cloves.

3. Butter both sides of the bread and cut it into strips.

4. Dred the strips in the egg mix and arrange them in your air fryer.

5. After two minutes of air frying, pause your air fryer, take out the pan, and spray the bread with a little cooking spray.

6. Once they're generously coated, flip and spray the other side, too.

7. Return them to the pan and cook for four more minutes. Check after a few minutes to make sure they're cooked evenly and not burning.

8. Once the egg is cooked through and the bread is golden, remove it and serve immediately with the icing sugar.

9. Top with a little whipped cream, maple syrup, or another garnish of your choice.

Breakfast Frittata

Serves: 2

Ingredients

- 3 Eggs
- ½ An Italian Sausage
- 4 Cherry Tomatoes, Halved
- 1 Tbsp. Olive Oil
- Parsley, Chopped
- Parmesan Cheese, Shredded
- Salt And Pepper

Directions

1. Preheat your air fryer to 360 degrees Fahrenheit.

2. Put the cherry tomatoes and the sausage in a baking pan and bake for five minutes.

3. In a bowl, whisk the rest of the ingredients together.

4. Remove the baking accessory from your air fryer and add the egg mix. Be sure it's in there evenly. Bake for another five minutes.

Easy Breakfast Sandwich

Serves: 1

Ingredients

- 1 Egg
- 1 Bacon Strip
- 1 English Muffin
- Salt And Pepper

Directions

1. Crack the egg into an oven proof bowl of soufflé cup.

2. Put the egg, bacon and the muffin into the air fryer.

3. Turn the air fryer to 395 degrees Fahrenheit for six minutes.

4. Assemble your sandwich and enjoy!

Baked Eggs with Parmesan, Bacon, and Tomatoes

Serves: 2

Ingredients

- 1 Slice Bacon
- 2 Eggs
- 2 Tbsp. Milk Or Heavy Cream
- 1 Tsp. Parmesan Cheese, Grated
- 1 Tsp. Tomato Sauce
- ½ Tsp. Pepper
- Parsley, To Garnish
- Two Slices Of Buttered Toast

Directions

1. Preheat your air fryer to 320 degrees Fahrenheit for three minutes.

2. Put the bacon in and cook it for nineteen minutes. Cut it into small pieces and divide the bacon equally between two ramekins.

3. Crack an egg into either ramekin and add a tablespoon of milk to each one.

4. Season the egg with some salt and pepper, add a bit of tomato sauce and divide it between each ramekin.

5. Sprinkle half a teaspoon of the parmesan cheese onto each mixture. Cook for eight minutes or until the yolk is slightly runny, or up to ten minutes for a hard yolk.

6. Top with the parsley to garnish and serve it with the toast.

One Dish Crustless Tomato and Onion Quiche

Serves: 2

Ingredients

- 2 Eggs
- ¼ C. Milk
- ½ C. Gouda Cheese, Shredded
- Salt
- ¼ C. Tomatoes, Diced
- 2 Tbsp. Onion, Diced

Directions

1. Put everything into a ramekin and whisk it together or use two smaller ramekins. Place it in an air fryer at 340 degrees Fahrenheit for twenty to thirty minutes, depending on what sized ramekin you used.

Baked Portobello Mushrooms

Serves: 4

Ingredients

- ½ Lb. Portobello Mushrooms, Caps Cleaned And Stalks Removed
- 1 ½ Oz. Mozzarella Cheese, Shredded
- 2 Slices Ham, Cubed
- 2 Button Mushrooms, Diced
- 1 Tbsp. Garlic, Chopped
- Salt And Pepper
- 4 Tbsp. Extra-Virgin Olive Oil
- Parsley

Directions

1. Brush the mushroom caps with half the olive oil and put them with the cap side down on a baking tray lined with some parchment paper.

2. Divide and top the mushrooms with cheese, ham, diced mushrooms, garlic, and a little salt and pepper. Drizzle the oil over the mushrooms.

3. Bake in a 320 degree Fahrenheit air fryer for ten minutes or until the cheese is bubbling and has become brown. Garnish with the parsley.

Eggs on Toast

Serves: 1

Ingredients

- 1 Slice Bread
- 1 Egg
- Balsamic Vinegar
- Maple Syrup
- Mozzarella Cheese, Shredded
- 1 Slice Bacon
- Italian Seasoning
- Salt
- 1 Tomato Slice
- Mayonnaise
- Butter

Directions

1. Lightly grease the ramekin with a piece of paper towel and the butter.

2. Line the dish with the bread and top with the sausage and tomato. Add the cheese.

3. Crack and egg over the top and add a few drops of vinegar and maple syrup. Season with the herbs and a little salt.

4. Top with more cheese if you'd like.

5. Bake at 320 degrees Fahrenheit for ten minutes in the air fryer. Squeeze a little mayonnaise over the top before serving.

Chapter Four - Lunch Recipes

Lunch can be made in just ten minutes to half an hour in your air fryer, and it's much healthier than a fast food hamburger and fries. Roast some vegetables for lunch and enjoy them with your favorite dressing, or even make an entire meal by air roasting a hamburger patty with some toppings.

Air Roasted Peppers

Serves: 3

Ingredients

- 1 Tbsp. Olive Oil
- 1 Tbsp. Maggi
- 1 Onion
- 12 Bell Peppers

Directions

1. Put the oil and the maggi in your air fryer pan.

2. Peel the onion and slice it into thin strips. Place that in the pan.

3. Prepare the peppers and slice them. Add them to the pan.

4. Cook for twenty-five minutes at 320 degrees Fahrenheit.

Grilled Endive in Curried Yogurt Marinade

Serves: 6

Ingredients

- 6 Heads Belgian Endive
- ½ C. Plain Fat-Free Yogurt
- 1 Tsp. Garlic Powder
- ½ Tsp. Curry Powder
- ½ Tsp. Salt
- ½ Tsp. Ground Black Pepper
- 3 Tbsp. Of Lemon Juice

Directions

1. Wash the endives and then cut them in half long ways through the root end. Set them aside to rest.

2. Mix the yogurt through the lemon juice in a bowl. Thin with a little more

lemon juice if you desire. Toss the endives into the marinades or brush them with it; it's your preference.

3. Cover and allow them to marinate for half an hour for up to twenty-four hours.

4. Cook for ten minutes in your air fryer at 360 degrees Fahrenheit.

Roasted Carrots

Serves: 4

Ingredients

- 1 Lb. Carrots
- 1 Tsp. Herbs De Provence
- 2 Tsp. Olive Oil
- 4 Tbsp. Orange Juice

Directions

1. Wash the carrots and dice. Don't peel them.

2. Put the carrots into the pan of your air fryer. Add the herbs and then top with the oil so that the herbs don't get blown around the air fryer.

3. Roast for twenty minutes at 320 degrees Fahrenheit.

4. Add the orange juice and roast another five minutes.

5. Serve hot.

Garlic and Vermouth Roasted Mushrooms

Serves: 4

Ingredients

- 2 Lbs. Mushrooms
- 1 Tbsp. Duck Fat
- ½ Tsp. Garlic Powder
- 2 Tsp. Herbs De Provence
- 2 Tbsp. White Vermouth

Directions

1. Wash the mushrooms and dry them gently with paper towels or in a salad spinner. Quarter them and set them aside.

2. Place the fat through the herbs de Provence in the pan of your air fryer and heat for two minutes. Stir with a wooden spoon if it clumps a bit. Add

the mushrooms and cook another twenty-five minutes. Add the vermouth and cook another five minutes.

Maple Glazed Roasted Parsnips

Serves: 6

Ingredients

- 2 Lbs. Parsnips
- 1 Tbsp. Duck Fat
- 1 Tbsp. Dried Parsley
- 2 Tbsp. Maple Syrup

Directions

1. Place the duck fat in the pan of a paddle-type air fryer and melt for two minutes.

2. Peel the parsnip and cut it into one inch or larger chunks. Place into the pan of the air fryer.

3. Cook for forty minutes and check it. Give it a little longer if the parsnip is not soft.

4. Sprinkle the parsley and drizzle with the maple syrup for the last five minutes of cooking.

Maple-Syrup Glazed Beets Air Roasted in Duck Fat

Serves: 8

Ingredients

- 3 ¼ Lbs. Beetroots
- 1 Tbsp. Duck Fat
- 4 Tbsp. Maple Syrup

Directions

1. Wash the beets gently and then peel them. Dice them into one-inch chunks.

2. Place the duck fat into the air fryer to melt it for a minute. Add the beetroot chunks and cook for forty minutes. Drizzle with two tablespoons of maple syrup and cook another ten minutes or until they're tender. Just before you serve them, toss in the last two tablespoons of maple syrup.

3. Serve hot.

Air-fried Zucchini Wedges

Serves: 4

Ingredients

- ½ C. Panko Crumbs
- ¼ C. Grated Parmesan
- ¼ Tsp. Basil
- ¼ Tsp. Oregano
- ¼ Tsp. Cayenne Pepper
- ¼ C. Egg White
- 2 Zucchini

Directions

1. In a bowl, mix the crumbs through the cayenne together and set it aside.

2. Wash the zucchini and leave it unpeeled. Cut it in half and then cut it into wedges not more than half an inch thick.

3. Spray the top rotating pan of your air fryer.

4. Place the egg white in a bowl and put a bit of the crumb mix on another plate. You only want to work with a bit of the crumb mix at a time because it will get matted and not useable.

5. Dip the zucchini wedges into the egg white and then into the crumb mixture. Press them down to get them coated well. Place the min the air fryer and repeat until all the wedges have been coated. Refill your crumb mixture as necessary.

6. Spray the wedges lightly with cooking spray in your air fryer. Cook for seven minutes and use tongs to turn them over. Cook another seven minutes and take them out. Cover and keep them warm as you do the second batch. Once you're ready to serve them, carefully add the first batch into

the air fryer a minute to get them nice and hot.

7. Serve each serving with some dipping sauce made from Greek yogurt and blue cheese or some ranch dressing.

Roasted Eggplant

Serves: 6

Ingredients

- 1 ½ Lbs. Eggplant
- 1 Tbsp. Duck Fat
- 1 Tbsp. Maggi Seasoning
- 1 Tsp. Onion Powder
- 1 Tsp. Garlic Powder
- 1 Tsp. Sumac
- 3 Tsp. Za'atar
- 2 Bay Leaves
- ½ A Lemon
- 1 Tsp. Olive Oil

Directions

1. Prepare the eggplant by washing it, stemming it, and cutting it into one-inch cubes. Set it aside and put

everything from the fat down to the bay leaves in your air fryer pan. Cook for two minutes to allow everything to incorporate well.

2. Add the eggplant to the air fryer.

3. Cook for twenty-five minutes.

4. In a bowl, mix the juice of half the lemon with a teaspoon of the olive oil. Dump the eggplant into it and toss it around.

5. Serve with a little parmesan cheese and fresh basil if you'd like.

Roasted Broccoli

Serves: 4

Ingredients

- 1 Head Of Broccoli
- 1 Tbsp. Duck Fat
- ½ Lemon
- 2 Tsp. Maggi
- 3 Garlic Cloves, Minced
- 2 Tbsp. White Sesame Seeds

Directions

1. Wash the broccoli, chop it into medium bite-sized pieces and spin it dry in a salad spinner, or you can pat it dry with some paper towels. Set it aside.

2. Peel and mince your garlic and set it aside.

3. Place into the air fryer one tablespoon of fat along with the juice of half a lemon. Add the Maggi and heat for two minutes. Add the garlic and the broccoli. Cook for thirteen minutes and sprinkle with a tablespoon of sesame seeds. Cook for the last five minutes to toast the sesame seeds.

Roasted Heritage Carrots and Rhubarb

Serves: 4

Ingredients

- 2 Tsp. Walnut Oil
- 1 Lb. Carrots
- 2 Lb. Rhubarb
- ½ Tsp. Sugar Substitute
- ½ C. Walnut Halves
- 1 Orange

Directions

1. Wash the carrots and dice them. Roast them in the oil in the air fryer for twenty minutes.

2. As the carrots are roasting, wash the rhubarb and dice it into half inch pieces. Chop the walnuts roughly and set them aside. Wash and zest your

orange and set the zest aside. Peel and section the orange and set those aside.

3. After the carrots have cooked, add the rhubarb through the walnuts and cook another five minutes.

4. Stir in two tablespoons of orange zest and the orange sections. Serve.

Chapter Five – Dinner Recipes

Many people come home from dinner and they're rushing around to get it ready. Wouldn't it be easier if you could just make dinner in one appliance that's so much easier to clean than your oven or stovetop? Well, you can with the air fryer! You can make patties for sandwiches, risottos your family will think a personal chef created, and even Asian cuisine they'll insist isn't unhealthy and full of fat, but everything you make in the air fryer will be free of excess fats! So go ahead, pop everything into the air fryer, turn it to half an hour, and enjoy your fifteen-minute cleanup afterward. It beats having to wash pot after pot.

Air-fried Turkey and Mushroom Patties

Serves: 5

Ingredients

- 6 Fresh Mushrooms, Pureed in a Food Processor

- 1 Tbsp. Maggi Seasoning

- 1 tsp. Garlic Powder

- 1 tsp. Onion Powder

- ½ tsp. Salt Substitute

- ½ tsp. Pepper

- 1 ¼ lbs. Extra-Lean Ground Turkey

Directions

1. Wash the mushrooms and shake off any excess water. Place them in the food processor and puree them.

2. Add the seasonings from the Maggi down to the pepper and pulse a few more times in the food processor.

3. Take out the mushrooms and put them in a bowl. Add the ground turkey and mix it well with your hands. Do not puree this in the food processor or it will make the turkey meat tough.

4. Divide the mix into five patties. Place an indent in the center of each patty with your thumb to keep it from making a football as you cook it.

5. Spray with a little cooking spray on both sides of the patties.

6. Put them in the basket of your air fryer and don't stack them. It's alright if the sides touch a little. Put the basket in and heat the air fryer to 320 degrees Fahrenheit. Cook them for ten minutes for them to be medium, or a little longer if you like them to be

well done. There's no need to turn them.

7. Serve them hot.

Air-Fried Meatloaf Slices

Serves: 4

Ingredients

- 4 Meatloaf Slices
- Cooking Spray

Directions

1. Cut the slices about an inch thick.

2. Turn each slice over gently and coat them with cooking spray on either side.

3. Use a spatula to slide them into the basket of the air fryer carefully. Don't stack them. It's alright if they touch a bit on the sides.

4. Air fry them for ten minutes or until they've browned and crisped a bit. Don't turn them over as they cook.

Green Curry Noodles

Serves: 6

Ingredients

- 2 Lbs. Shirataki Noodles
- 2 Tbsp. Soy Sauce
- 1 ½ Tbsp. Fish Sauce
- 1 Tsp. Sesame Oil
- ½ Tsp. Garlic Powder
- 12 Oz. Tofu
- 5 Oz. Snow Peas
- 1 Red Pepper, Sliced
- 1 Green Pepper, Sliced
- ½ Lb. Mushrooms, Sliced
- 1 C. Water Chestnuts, Sliced
- 1 Tsp. Coriander Paste
- 3 Tbsp. Lime Juice

- 2 Tsp. Lemon Grass Paste
- 4 Tbsp. Rice Vinegar
- 12 Oz. Napa Cabbage
- 2 Carrot, Shredded
- 4 Spring Onions, Chopped
- 12 Shrimp, Cooked
- 6 Tbsp. Thai Green Curry Paste

Directions

1. If your noodles came packed in water, drain them in a sieve and rinse them with some fresh water. Then put them in a heatproof bowl with two cups of water and a tablespoon of soy sauce. Stir them with a fork and set them aside.

2. Make the marinade from three tablespoons of soy sauce through the garlic powder. Cut the tofu into chunks about half an inch thick. Put it into a bowl with the marinade and

toss it. Then set it aside as you prepare the following step.

3. Prepare the stir fry vegetables from the snow peas down to the water chestnuts. Add a little broccoli if you'd like. Set the mixture aside.

4. Make the dressing by mixing together the coriander paste through the lemon grass paste. Add four tablespoons of the Thai paste and two tablespoons of the rice vinegar. Set this aside.

5. Shred the cabbage, wash and shred the carrot, and mince the spring onion. Set them aside. You can add a little fresh, chopped cucumber at this point if you'd like.

6. Spray the bottom of your air fryer bowl with cooking spray and remove the tofu cubes to the bowl using a slotted spoon. Spray the cubes a bit and then cook for thirteen minutes or until they begin to crisp. Tip them into

a bowl or a plate and cover them to keep them warm.

7. Repeat the above step with the shrimp but only cook for five minutes. Remove them and set them aside. Cover and keep them warm.

8. Make a stir fry sauce by using the leftover marinade, the rest of the vinegar, and the rest of the Thai curry paste. Stir briefly to blend it and then empty it into the air fryer bowl. Tip the stir fry vegetables in and spray them lightly with some cooking spray. Cook for five minutes.

9. In a bowl or pot, put the drained noodles, dressing, and tofu cubes in. Add the stir fry vegetables and any sauce that's leftover. Add the fresh vegetables and toss with some tongs. Put the shrimp in and serve it by dividing it into six bowls.

Air-fried Burgers

Serves: 4

Ingredients

- 1 Tbsp. Worcestershire Sauce
- 1 Tsp. Maggi Seasoning
- 2 Drops Liquid Smoke
- ½ Tsp. Onion Powder
- ½ Tsp. Garlic Powder
- ½ Tsp. Salt Substitute
- ½ Tsp. Pepper
- ½ Tsp. Dried Oregano
- 1 Tsp. Parsley
- 1 Lb. Extra-Lean Ground Beef

Directions

1. Spray the upper tray of your air fryer and set it aside.

2. In a bowl, mix the seasonings together from the Worcestershire sauce down to the parsley.

3. Add this and the beef in a bowl.

4. Mix it together well but be careful not to overmix the beef as it will make tough burgers.

5. Divide the beef into four patties and shape with your hands. With your thumb, make an indent in the center of each patty to keep them from pushing up in the center.

6. Put the tray into the air fryer and spray the tops of the patties lightly with cooking spray.

7. Cook for ten minutes for medium doneness or for fifteen for well done. There's no need to turn them.

8. Serve them on a hot bun with a side dish of your choice.

Roasted Vegetable Pasta Salad

Serves: 16

Ingredients

- 3 Eggplants
- 1 Tbsp. Olive Oil
- 3 Zucchinis
- 1 Tbsp. Olive Oil
- 4 Tomatoes, Quartered Into Eighths
- 4 C. Pasta, Uncooked
- 2 Bell Peppers
- 1 C. Cherry Tomatoes, Sliced
- 2 Tsp. Salt Substitute
- 8 Tbsp. Parmesan Cheese, Grated
- ½ C. Fat-Free Italian Dressing
- 3 Basil Leaves

Directions

1. Wash the eggplant and slice off the green ends. Don't peel the eggplant. Slice it into half inch rounds. If you're using a paddle-type air fryer, put one tablespoon of oil into the pan along with the eggplant. If you're using a basket-type air fryer, then toss in a tablespoon of oil and then add the eggplant to the basket. Cook for forty minutes or until the eggplant is soft and there isn't a bitter taste left. Set it aside.

2. Wash the zucchini and slice off the green ends. Don't peel them. Slice them into half inch thick rounds. If you're using the air fryer that's a paddle type, then put the oil into the pan along with the zucchini. If you're using a basket-type, then put the oil in the proper place and put the zucchini into the basket. Cook for twenty-five minutes or until it's soft. Set it aside.

3. Wash the tomatoes and quarter them, cutting each quarter into another half. If you're using an air fryer with a grill pan, then arrange the tomatoes on that and spray them lightly with cooking spray. If you're using a basket air fryer, arrange them in that and spray lightly with the cooking spray. Roast for half an hour or until they're reduced in size and just beginning to brown. Set them aside.

4. Cook the pasta according to its directions and empty it into a colander. Run cool water over it to wash off a little starch and drain it. Then set it aside to cool.

5. Wash and seed the bell pepper and put it into a bowl. Wash and slice the cherry tomatoes and add them to the bowl. Add the roasted vegetables, pasta, salt, dressing, and some chopped basil. Then mix in the parmesan and toss it well.

6. Allow it to chill and marinate in the refrigerator. Serve chilled.

Pasta Sauce

Serves: 6

Ingredients

- 1 Tbsp. Oil
- 1 Onion
- 2 Bell Peppers
- ½ Lb. Mushrooms
- 3 Lbs. Tomatoes
- 5.5 Oz. Tomato Paste
- Herbs Of Your Choice

Directions

1. Prepare the vegetables by slicing the mushrooms and setting them aside. Wash seed and slice your bell peppers. Set them aside. Peel the onion and slice it into rings. Cut the rings in half and set the onion aside.

2. Heat the oil in your air fryer for two minutes.

3. Add the onion and cook it for five minutes.

4. Add the green pepper and cook it another ten minutes.

5. Add the mushrooms and cook them another fifteen minutes.

6. Puree the tomatoes in a blender if they're fresh and add them to the air fryer.

7. Add the herbs, such as basil, oregano, and marjoram. Add the tomato paste and stir in the herbs so they don't get blown around.

8. Cook another sixty-five minutes.

Barley, Mushroom, and Sweet Potato Risotto

Serves: 8

Ingredients

- 2 Onions, Chopped
- 2 Garlic Cloves, Chopped
- 3 Tbsp. Oil
- 5 C. Stock
- 2 Lbs. Sweet Potatoes, Peeled And Diced
- ¾ Lb. Pearl Barley
- 1 Can Mushrooms, Sliced
- ¼ C. Parmesan Cheese
- 3 Oz. Fat-Free Milk
- 1 Tsp. Thyme
- 1 Tsp. Tarragon

Directions

1. Bring the stock to boil in a saucepan or boil it in the microwave.

2. Put the sweet potato in the air fryer with two tablespoons of oil and cook for ten minutes. Add the onion and garlic and cook another five minutes. Add the barley and cook another five minutes.

3. Then add four cups of the hot stock to the air fryer and cook for half an hour. After half an hour, adjust the liquid level to your preference with the reserved stock and add the mushrooms, milk, cheese, and herbs. Cook another five to seven minutes.

Turkey and Beer Risotto

Serves: 6

Ingredients

- 2 Onions, Chopped
- 2 Tbsp. Oil
- 2 Cans Mushrooms
- 1 Tsp. Oregano
- 1 Tsp. Basil
- 1 Tbsp. Oil
- 1 ½ C. Risotto
- 2 C. Beer
- 2 C. Turkey, Chopped
- 5 C. Stock, Heated
- 1 Tbsp. Butter
- ½ C. Parmesan Cheese, Grated

Directions

1. Heat the stock and set it aside.

2. Chop the onions and toss them into the air fryer with two tablespoons of oil. Cook them for five minutes.

3. Add the mushrooms, oregano, and basil and cook another ten minutes.

4. Add another tablespoon of oil and the rice. Cook for five minutes.

5. Add the beer and cook another five minutes.

6. Add the turkey along with five cups of stock and cook another twenty-five minutes. Add the tablespoon of butter and the cheese and cook another five minutes.

7. Serve with parmesan cheese over the top.

Faux Fried Rice

Serves: 8

Ingredients

- 1 Tbsp. Sesame Oil
- 1 Tbsp. Peanut Oil
- 4 Tbsp. Soy Sauce
- 4 Garlic Cloves, Minced
- 1 Tbsp. Ginger, Minced
- ½ Lemon, Juiced
- 1 Cauliflower Head
- 1 Can Water Chestnuts, 8 Oz.
- ¾ C. Peas
- 2 Cans Mushrooms, 16 Oz.
- ½ C. Egg Substitute

Directions

1. Place the ingredients up to the lemon juice in the air fryer bowl.

2. Peel the cauliflower and wash it. Cut it into small florets and don't leave any in large pieces. Put them into the bowl of a food processor, a few at a time and mince them until they resemble rice or wheat grain. Empty that into the air fryer bowl and repeat until all the cauliflower has been processed.

3. Drain the can of water chestnuts and chop it coarsely. Add it to the air fryer.

4. Turn the air fryer on and cook it for twenty minutes. After twenty minutes, add the peas and the mushrooms. Allow that to cook another fifteen minutes. In a frying pan sprayed with a little cooking oil, cook the half a cup of egg substitute to make an omelet. Turn it onto a cutting board and chop

it up. Add it to the rice mix and cook another five minutes.

Healthy Yakitori

Serves: 4

Ingredients

- 4 Pieces Chicken Thigh Meat
- 5 Spring Onions
- ¼ C. Soy Sauce
- 1 Tsp. Sugar
- 1 Tbsp. Mirin
- 1 Tsp. Garlic Salt
- 8 (6") Bamboo Skewers

Directions

1. Soak the bamboo in water for fifteen minutes.

2. Cut the chicken into one-inch pieces.

3. Cut the spring onions into one-inch lengths. Stick the chicken and onion on the sticks, alternating in order.

4. Make the marinade by mixing the soy sauce through the garlic salt together.

5. Marinate the chicken for three hours.

6. Air fry the skewers for ten to twelve minutes at 350 degrees Fahrenheit.

Chapter Six – Air Fryer Snack Recipes

Everyone can go for a snack, especially when they know their foods are restricted by some sort of diet, but the air fryer can turn your favorite snacks into something you can enjoy without feeling guilty. Fry up a batch of air-fried potato chips or sweet potato chips and enjoy the crunch as you watch your favorite movie!

Cheese Rice Balls

Serves: 2

Ingredients

- 1 C. Boiled Rice
- 1 C. Paneer, Grated
- 2 Tbsp. Carrots, Grated
- Mozzarella Cheese
- 1 Green Chili, Minced
- 1 Tbsp. Corn Starch
- 1 Tbsp. Corn Starch And 4 Tbsp. Water Mixed
- Bread Crumbs
- Garlic Powder
- Oregano
- Salt And Pepper

Directions

1. In a bowl, mix the rice and paneer. Season with the garlic powder, oregano, and salt and pepper. Mash it together to make the dough.

2. Mix the carrot, mozzarella cheese, cornstarch, and chili to make a filling.

3. Stuff the carrot mixture into the dough and make a ball. Dip the ball in the cornstarch and water mixture and roll them in the breadcrumbs. Air fry for ten to fifteen minutes at 200 degrees Fahrenheit. Serve hot with tomato sauce.

Cheese Paneer Balls

Serves: 4

Ingredients

- 7 Oz. Paneer Cheese, Grated
- 1 ¾ Oz. Cheese, Cubed
- 2 Tbsp. Gram Flour
- 1 Tbsp. Corn Starch
- 2 Onions, Minced
- 1 Green Chili, Minced
- 1" Ginger, Minced
- ½ Tsp. Red Chili Powder
- Coriander Leaves, Chopped
- Oil For Frying
- Salt To Taste

Directions

1. Mix everything together but the cheese and oil. Take a small bit and roll it into your palm and make it like a pancake, flat. Stuff a cheese cube inside and seal the edges to make a ball by rolling it in the palm of your hand. Repeat with the rest of the cheese.

2. Air fry for ten to fifteen minutes at 200 degrees Fahrenheit. Serve hot with green chutney.

Crispy Potato Skin Wedges

Serves: 4

Ingredients

- 4 Medium Potatoes
- 1 C. Water
- 3 Tbsp. Oil
- 1 Tsp. Paprika
- ¼ Tsp. Pepper
- ¼ Tsp. Salt

Directions

1. Scrub the potatoes to clean them and boil them in salted water for forty minutes or until they're fork tender. Cool them half an hour in the refrigerator.

2. In a bowl, mix the oil through the pepper together. Cut the cooled potato into quarters and toss them

into the mixture of oil and spices. Preheat your air fryer to 390 degrees Fahrenheit and add half the potato wedges to your basket.

3. Put the skin side down and be careful not to overcrowd them. Cook them for thirteen to fifteen minutes for each batch or until they're golden brown.

Cheddar Bacon Croquettes

Serves: 6

Ingredients

- 1 lb. cheddar cheese
- 1 lb. bacon
- 2 tbsp. olive oil
- 1 c. flour
- 2 eggs, beaten
- ½ c. seasoned breadcrumbs

Directions

1. Cut the cheddar cheese block into six equal portions, about an inch wide. Take two pieces of bacon and wrap them around a piece of cheese. Enclose the cheese entirely. Trim off any excess fat from the bacon. Put the cheddar into the freezer for five minutes to firm it, but don't freeze it.

2. Preheat your air fryer to 390 degrees Fahrenheit and mix the oil and breadcrumbs together. Stir until the mix is loose and crumbly. Put the cheddar blocks in flour, then the eggs, and finally the breadcrumbs. Press them to ensure the breadcrumbs adhere to the croquettes. Place them in the basket for seven to eight minutes or until they're golden.

Feta Triangles

Serves: 5

Ingredients

- 1 Egg Yolk
- 4 Oz. Feta Cheese
- 2 Tbsp. Parsley, Chopped
- 1 Scallion, Minced
- 5 Sheets Filo Pastry
- 2 Tbsp. Olive Oil
- Pepper

Directions

1. Beat the egg in a bowl and mix in the feta through the scallion. Season with pepper to taste. Cut the filo dough into three strips and scoop a teaspoon of the feta mixture onto the underside of the strip puff pastry. Fold

the pastry over the filling to make a triangle.

2. Preheat your air fryer to 390 degrees Fahrenheit and brush the filo with a bit of oil. Put five triangles in your cooking basket and cook for three minutes in the air fryer. Repeat with the rest of the triangles.

Jerk Chicken Wings

Serves: 6

Ingredients

- 4 Lbs. Chicken Wings
- 2 Tbsp. Olive Oil
- 2 Tbsp. Soy Sauce
- 6 Garlic Cloves, Minced
- 1 Habanero Pepper, Deseeded And Minced
- 1 Tbsp. Allspice
- 1 Tsp. Cinnamon
- 1 Tsp. Cayenne Pepper
- 1 Tsp. White Pepper
- 1 Tsp. Salt
- 2 Tbsp. Brown Sugar
- 1 Tbsp. Thyme, Minced

- 1 Tbsp. Ginger, Grated
- 4 Scallions, Minced
- 5 Tbsp. Lime Juice
- ½ C. Red Wine Vinegar

Directions

1. In a mixing bowl, combine everything and cover the chicken thoroughly with the seasonings to marinade. Transfer to a one-gallon bag and refrigerate for at least two hours or up to twenty-four hours.

2. Preheat your air fryer to 390 degrees Fahrenheit and remove the wings from the bag. Drain away all the liquid. Pat them dry with a paper towel. Put half the wings in the cooking basket and cook the batches for fourteen to sixteen minutes each. Serve with blue cheese dressing or ranch dressing.

Cajun Shrimp

Serves: 2

Ingredients

- ½ Lb. Tiger Shrimp, 16-20 Shrimp

- ¼ Tsp. Cayenne Pepper

- ½ Tsp. Old Bay Seasoning

- ¼ Tsp. Smoke Paprika

- 1 Pinch Of Salt

- 1 Tbsp. Olive Oil

Directions

1. Preheat your air fryer to 390 degrees Fahrenheit. In a bowl, combine all the ingredients and coat the shrimp with the oil and spices. Put the shrimp in the basket and cook for five minutes. Serve over rice.

Air Fried Gourmet Potato Chips

Serves: 2

Ingredients

- 2 ¼ Lbs. Potatoes
- 1 Tbsp. Duck Fat
- Maldon Salt

Directions

1. Wash and peel your potatoes. Slice them thinly. If you have a mandolin, then use it. Put the potatoes into a large pot of cool water and soak them for a few minutes. This protects them from discoloring due to the air and leeches out extra starch to make a crispier potato chip. Swirl it around a bit to help remove the starch.

2. Place the duck fat in the air fryer and heat for two minutes.

3. Drain the potato slices and pat them dry with a paper towel or tea towel.

4. Add them to the air fryer bowl and spread them out evenly.

5. Cook for forty to fifty minutes at ten-minute intervals. At the end of every interval, use some tongs to break apart the clumps and spread them out.

6. Transfer them to a bowl and toss them with a few pinches of Maldon salt.

Crispy Jalapeno Poppers

Serves: 1

Ingredients

- 2 Jalapeno Peppers
- 1 Oz. Cheddar Cheese
- 1 Spring Roll Wrapper
- 1 Tbsp. Egg Beaters

Directions

1. Prepare the peppers by chopping off the stem, slicing them long ways, and trimming out the white pith and seeds. Rinse them under water to get rid of any stubborn seeds and pat them dry. Try to keep the matching halves together as you'll be putting them back together.

2. Divide the cheese into two half ounce strips.

3. Peel off a sheet of the spring roller wrapper and cut it in half. Brush the halves with a tablespoon of egg mix.

4. Put half the jalapeno in one corner of the wrapper with the egg brushed side facing up. Put a strip of cheese in the jalapeno and top with the other half of the jalapeno pepper.

5. Hold the two halves together as you roll up the pepper tightly in the wrapper, folding the edges in as you go.

6. Once you're finished, do a check for any loose seems. Glue any you find down with a little egg brushed on the edges.

7. Once it's assembled, give the poppers a light spray with cooking spray and turn them over to do the other side.

8. Put them on the top tray of the air fryer and turn it on for ten minutes.

There isn't any need to turn them as you cook them.

9. Serve hot with marinara sauce.

Sweet Potato Fries

Serves: 2

Ingredients

- 2 Large Sweet Potatoes
- 1 Tbsp. Oil

Directions

1. Wash the sweet potatoes and peel them. Rinse them once again to get rid of any leftover dirt or peel.

2. Cut them into chips or fries and put them into a large bowl.

3. Add a tablespoon of oil to the bowl and use your hands to toss them well. You might want to have the air fryer basket pulled out and sitting beside you so you don't have to wash your oily hands and then touch the fries again.

4. Cook them at 320 degrees Fahrenheit for fifteen minutes.

5. Take the fries out and tip them back into the bowl you were using. Toss them to get some extra oil on them and use a large spoon to coat them.

6. Transfer them back to the fryer basket and put them back in the machine. Raise the temperature to 350 degrees Fahrenheit. Cook another five minutes.

7. Take them out, tip them back into the bowl, and toss them again.

8. Transfer them back to the air fryer basket and leave them temperature the same. Roast another five minutes, and serve hot.

Chapter Seven – Troubleshooting Your Air Fryer

Using your air fryer should be pretty easy, but there are some complications that might come up. In this chapter, we're going to explore the common concerns and questions many have when they first get their air fryer.

Not Enough Crispiness

Most of the common air fryer complications are issues that pertain to the texture of the foods cooked in the appliance. Some owners complain their final product is chewy, soggy, or too dry. The one thing it's not is crispy! And when you serve things like fried chicken or French fries, most people like a little crunch. So what's the solution?

There are a few different reasons as to why your air fryer might not be crisping as it should. Despite the name, most air fryers do best when only a light coating of oil is applied to the food before it's cooked. It's possible to make foods like fries and fried chicken without using any oil, but most manufacturers and recipes recommend a bit of oil if you want to achieve the optimal results.

Prepared, oven ready fries and snacks work the best in an air fryer. Frozen dumplings, spring rolls, and croquettes will turn out delicious when you use your air fryer to prepare them. That's because they usually include oil or fat in the precooked product.

Homemade fries can be made in the air fryer, but a few rules should be followed if you want to be crispy and crunchy like truly fried fries.

1. Soak the cut potatoes in some cold water for twenty minutes to remove starch.

2. Dry your uncooked fries with a paper towels or a clean tea towel to remove any excess water.

3. Give them a gentle spritz of vegetable oil or olive oil and season them with your salt and pepper before frying.

4. Preheat your air fryer before you add the ingredients.

5. Put the fries in the basket and cook them. The cooking time is going to

depend on the amount of fries and the individual model's specifications.

And there you have it, a low-fat alternative to the traditional fries that have spent way too long in unhealthy fat and oil. If your food seems to be unevenly cooked, remember you might need to give the basket a shake every now and again according to the manufacturer's instructions. This will keep the hot air circulating evenly around the ingredients in the air fryer.

Another good tip is to not stack or overload the items that are in the air fryer.

Black Smoke

If you see black smoke coming out of your air fryer, promptly unplug it from the outlet. Once the smoke has stopped, remove the basket or the pan from the appliance. The heating element might have been damaged or a circuit might have shorted inside the unit somewhere.

So what's the solution?

Find a service center that knows how to fix air fryers.

Be sure they're certified by the manufacturer to perform repairs on that make and model of air fryer unit. If the unit is still covered by the warranty, it might be viable to fix the air fryer. Broken air fryers with expired warranties might not be worth fixing. You might just want to get a new air fryer.

White Smoke

If there's excessive amounts of oil or fat in the foods you're preparing in the air fryer, white smoke or mist might sometimes be seen coming out of the appliance. This isn't usually dangerous, but it can be disturbing.

The solution?

Try to avoid cooking any high-fat foods. Fatty meats like sausage tend to cause white smoke. When you go to select cuts of meat to prepare in the air fryer, try finding the amount of fat contained in the cut of meat or the prepackaged food. Opt for the lowest amount of fat you can find.

Power Supply Problems

Is your air fryer switched on but it's not turning on? Sometimes the air fryer not heating up right can mean there's an issue with the wiring in the unit, but before you panic, be sure to plug it into another outlet to make sure it's not the outlet it's plugged into. It's worth checking the circuit breaker, too. Check to make sure the timer hasn't been set. Some units can be programmed to stay off until a certain time. If the fryer is still under warranty, then take it to see a technician or return it to the manufacturer for a replacement.

Tips and Tricks for Operation

Here are a few more tips to operating your air fryer properly before you get started!

1. When preparing fried food, add just a bit of oil to the food and oil spray the bottom of the mesh cooking basket to keep things from sticking. Be sure you use enough space between the edge of the basket and the ingredients, too. You should have half an inch of space around the bottom edge of your basket and space between food pieces.

2. Pat your foods dry to avoid splattering and excessive white smoke. Be sure to empty the fat out of the bottom of the machine after each use.

3. Before you begin cooking, preheat your air fryer for three minutes if the recipe doesn't instruct you to put the ingredients in right away. In addition,

make sure the air fryer has reached your desired cooking temperature.

4. Never overcrowd the ingredients in the basket or you will increase the cooking time and cause foods to come out raw. Give enough space between the foods to make sure the air can circulate evenly.

5. Prepackaged foods can be made in the air fryer by lowering the conventional oven temperate by seventy degrees Fahrenheit. Reduce the cooking time to half and remember that time and temperature can vary between foods. Always check them with a thermometer to make sure they're done.

6. While you're using the air fryer, always be sure to shake the cooking basket. Smaller items like fries and wings should be shook a few times. Rotate the items every five to ten

minutes to ensure the food cooks evenly.

7. Empty the fat out of the bottom of the air fryer, especially if you're making foods naturally high in fat, like chicken wings. This will help you avoid excessive white smoke, too.

8. Be sure you clean the air fryer basket and pan after every use. If you don't, the kitchen will smell like fried foods. You want to loosen any food particles on the cooking basket by soaking it in soapy water prior to scrubbing it gently or putting it in the dishwasher.

9. To clean the outside and inside of the air fryer, clean the outside with a moist cloth and the inside with a sponge soaked in hot water. Clean the heating element with a soft bristle brush only and dry it with paper towels. Never use a steel wire brush or a hard bristled brush.

Conclusion

Remember to look at the features of the models available before you purchase your air fryer to determine which one is best for you. In addition to features, always be sure to read reviews and the manufacturer's warranty to make sure you're purchasing a model that's proven to last with daily use. You're going to love your new air fryer, so you'll be guaranteed to use it often. That means you want one that will stick with you for a long time, unlike the plaque in your arteries from traditional fried foods.

If you enjoyed the information you found in this book about air fryers, please leave a review at your online eBook retailer's website. Every review counts and helps more people find valuable information that will help them.

Thank you for reading!

30558444R00069

Made in the USA
San Bernardino, CA
16 February 2016